GROWING UP

BY DUCHESS HARRIS, JD, PHD

WITH REBECCA ROWELL

CONTENT CONSULTANT

HEATH FOGG DAVIS, PHD
DIRECTOR, GENDER, SEXUALITY,
AND WOMEN'S STUDIES PROGRAM
TEMPLE UNIVERSITY

Essential Library

An Imprint of Abdo Publishing | abdobooks.com

ABDOBOOKS.COM

Published by Abdo Publishing, a division of ABDO, PO Box 398166, Minneapolis, Minnesota 55439. Copyright © 2020 by Abdo Consulting Group, Inc. International copyrights reserved in all countries. No part of this book may be reproduced in any form without written permission from the publisher. Essential Library™ is a trademark and logo of Abdo Publishing.

Printed in the United States of America, North Mankato, Minnesota.
042019
092019

Cover Photo: Stephen Orsillo/Shutterstock Images
Interior Photos: Bob Andres/Atlanta Journal-Constitution/AP Images, 4–5; Shutterstock Images, 7, 13, 35, 41, 43, 48, 62, 97; Rachael Warriner/Shutterstock Images, 10; Amy Harris/Invision/AP Images, 15; ABC/Photofest, 16; Dean Mitchell/iStockphoto, 19; Sam Killerman/It'sPronouncedMetrosexual.com/The Genderbread Person, 20; iStockphoto, 24–25, 65, 77, 86; Robert Perry/Getty Images News/Getty Images, 29; Sorbis/Shutterstock Images, 31; Beatriz Vera/Shutterstock Images, 38; Wave Break Media/Shutterstock Images, 50–51; Jordan Strauss/Invision for Buzzfeed/AP Images, 55; Elaine Thompson/AP Images, 57; Nam Y. Huh/AP Images, 60; SolStock/iStockphoto, 67; Rawpixel/iStockphoto, 68; FX Network/Photofest, 71; Kevin Winter/Getty Images Entertainment/Getty Images, 73; Richard Green/Alamy, 79; Carlos David/Shutterstock Images, 81; Pixel-Shot/Shutterstock Images, 84; Jill Richardson/Shutterstock Images, 91; Somsak Nitimongkolchai/Shutterstock Images, 93

Editor: Megan Ellis
Series Designer: Melissa Martin

LIBRARY OF CONGRESS CONTROL NUMBER: 2018966049

PUBLISHER'S CATALOGING-IN-PUBLICATION DATA

Names: Harris, Duchess, author. | Rowell, Rebecca, author.
Title: Growing up LGBTQ / by Duchess Harris and Rebecca Rowell
Description: Minneapolis, Minnesota : Abdo Publishing, 2020 | Series: Being LGBTQ in America | Includes online resources and index.
Identifiers: ISBN 9781532119040 (lib. bdg.) | ISBN 9781532173226 (ebook)
Subjects: LCSH: LGBTQ people--Juvenile literature. | Sexual minority community--Juvenile literature. | Homosexuality--Psychological aspects--Juvenile literature. | Coming out (Sexual identity)--Juvenile literature.
Classification: DDC 306.76--dc23

CONTENTS

1

HOMECOMING
FOR SAGE LOVELL

On October 17, 2014, many students at Walton High School in Marietta, Georgia, attended their school's homecoming football game. During halftime, the homecoming queen and princesses walked onto the field. The crowd cheered and clapped for the young women. Sage Lovell, a junior, was one of them. She wore a magenta gown and held a bouquet of red roses. Lovell's father was dressed in a tuxedo. He escorted her onto the field. The expression on his face as he looked at his daughter was one of love and pride. The scene looked like any other homecoming, but it was not. Lovell was the first transgender, or trans, student elected to a homecoming court in Georgia history. Someone who is trans has a gender identity that is different from the sex they were assigned at birth.

Lovell was in her homeroom class when she found out she had been elected to the homecoming court. She was one of 50 girls vying for a spot on the homecoming court. Her classmates cheered when they heard the news. Lovell spoke with a reporter at CBS 46, a news station in Atlanta, about her experience being elected homecoming princess. "Apparently [the cheer] was able to be heard from across the school," Lovell explained.[1]

SUPPORT FROM FRIENDS AND FAMILY

Lovell's friends had always supported her. So had her parents. Lovell was assigned male at birth. In middle school, Lovell realized she was attracted to boys. She came out as gay when she was in the

SOUTHERN STORIES

In 2014, GLAAD conducted a poll about people's thoughts regarding LGBTQ Americans. The survey results revealed that, even with recent strides in LGBTQ civil rights and legislation, many people in the United States remained uneasy with having LGBTQ family and community members. The survey found that this discomfort is particularly strong among people who live in the South, more so than for respondents from other areas of the country.

In response to the survey results, GLAAD introduced the series Southern Stories to share the experiences of LGBTQ people in the South. GLAAD explains on its website that the goal of Southern Stories is "to create a cultural shift towards LGBTQ acceptance and understanding in the region."[2] The stories focus on everyday people and the highs and lows they face related to identifying as LGBTQ. One of the first stories GLAAD published was about Sage Lovell.

Homecoming dances are a popular activity among high school students.

ninth grade. According to Lovell, her friends were not surprised. Soon, Lovell realized that she was also a girl.

In 2014, Lovell and her family spoke with Claire Pires of GLAAD, a nonprofit that focuses on lesbian, gay, bisexual, transgender, and queer (LGBTQ) representation in the media. Lovell's mom, Maureen, said of her daughter, "She's very inspiring to me, just the bravery that she shows to truly be herself." Lovell's dad, Joseph, spoke about homecoming and walking his daughter onto the football field: "The experience on the football field was awesome. There was so much support, so much excitement. . . . It was phenomenal."[3]

THE HOMECOMING EXPERIENCE

For Lovell, being a homecoming princess was unforgettable. She said:

Being on homecoming court was the first time that I have ever done anything so definitively feminine, something that, at least within my school, is an undisputed female role. It helped me cement my place as a woman to myself and the world.[4]

But Lovell's experience was more than a personal one. Media stories about her helped bring awareness of her experience to her community. She hoped that awareness would reach a broad area of the American South. Lovell said, "I hope that people saw one of my articles and did some research on trans people and found positive information and changed their viewpoint."[5]

Lovell also saw the possibility of what her story could mean for other transgender youth. She hoped to be an example for them and encourage them to be themselves and even to run for homecoming court. Lovell summed up her homecoming experience this way: "All in all my goal was to make a mark,

HOMECOMING COURT AGAIN

In October 2015, Sage Lovell again had the support of her classmates during homecoming. They elected her to the homecoming court a second time. The senior became one of five girls to be considered for homecoming queen. She did not win homecoming queen but was supportive of her friend who did. Lovell spoke about being reelected: "There was less reaction than last year probably because it's 'old news.' I kind of broke the barrier down last year. People were super happy and excited that I was on there and nothing negative was said to my face."[6]

Some LGBTQ youth display their gender identity or sexual orientation with flags. The transgender flag is blue, pink, and white.

even if a small one, and to help transgender visibility and future progression. I believe I have done that."[7]

GROWING UP LGBTQ

Lovell is one of many young people in the United States who identify as LGBTQ. Like other LGBTQ youth, she has coped with her identity and self-expression, coming out, and activism in her own way. Young people in the LGBTQ community also often face other challenges, such as bullying, discrimination, and mental health issues.

Being an LGBTQ youth is not a singular experience. It is different for everyone. Understanding the experiences of LGBTQ youth can help those youth as they strive to become healthy, happy adults. Such understanding can also help others by providing awareness about what it means to grow up identifying with the LGBTQ community.

DISCUSSION STARTERS

- Why did Sage Lovell's story make the news in her hometown? Why is it important to recognize people who are the first to do something?

- Have you won any awards or recognitions at your school? How did that make you feel?

- Sage Lovell's classmates cheered when she was elected to homecoming court. What are other ways to show support for LGBTQ classmates?

Some people understand their identity at a young age. For other people, understanding may take well into adulthood.

WHAT IT MEANS
TO BE LGBTQ

Sage Lovell is part of the LGBTQ community. Understanding the issues of growing up LGBTQ in America—and those of the community as a whole—first requires understanding what being LGBTQ means. People in the LGBTQ community have gender identities or sexual orientations that are outside the societal norm. They may also be part of other minority groups. However, what unites people in the LGBTQ community is the shared experience of discrimination based on violating specific societal norms.

SEXUAL ORIENTATION

Sexual orientation is a person's attraction to certain genders of other people. *Gay*, *lesbian*, and *bisexual* are all sexual orientations. So are *pansexual*, *asexual*, and *heterosexual*. Someone who is gay is attracted to people of the same gender. The attraction may be emotional, romantic, or sexual. Some women who are attracted to women prefer to be called *lesbian*.

Someone who is attracted to the same gender and also other genders may prefer to be called *bisexual* or *pansexual*. A person can also be asexual, or without sexual attraction.

The term *queer* is often used instead of *LGBTQ*. It was once used as a slur against LGBTQ people. Now it is used as an umbrella, or group, term to refer to many people in the LGBTQ community. Some people also identify with *queer* personally instead of other labels for their gender identity or sexuality.

Growing up, people with sexual orientations other than heterosexual may have trouble seeing themselves represented in pop culture. Singer Hayley Kiyoko, who identifies as a lesbian, recalls watching the show *Grey's Anatomy* as a kid just for bisexual

SAME-GENDER LOVING

Not all people use the same labels to define their sexuality or gender identity. White men began to use *gay* in the 1950s to replace the word *homosexual*, which was used by medical professionals who wanted to "cure" their sexual orientation. White women began using the term *lesbian*, which they took from the Greek island Lesbos. The ancient Greek poet Sappho lived on Lesbos and wrote many poems about her love for women.

Some black people may use the label *same-gender loving* instead of *gay* or *lesbian*. This term was coined in the 1990s as a way for black men and women to identify both their sexuality and their culture. According to the magazine *Urban Socialites*, the term "was introduced to enhance the lives and amplify the voices of homosexual and bi-sexual" black people. It adds that the term "provide[s] a powerful identification not marginalized by racism in the gay community or by 'homophobic' attitudes in society at large."[1]

Hayley Kiyoko writes and performs many songs that reference her sexual orientation.

Callie Torres, *left*, on *Grey's Anatomy* was played by actress Sara Ramirez. Ramirez is openly bisexual.

character Callie Torres. Kiyoko hopes that she provides that same representation to young girls when she performs onstage. She adds, "If they can see me flirt with girls on stage, then they can be like, 'Oh, I can do that too, I can get a girl like that, those feelings are normal.'"[2]

GENDER IDENTITY

Gender identity is a person's inner experience of their gender. This may be male, female, neither, or somewhere in the middle. A cisgender, or cis, person has a gender identity that matches the sex they were assigned at birth. A trans person has a different gender identity than what they were assigned at birth.

Many Western countries such as the United States adhere to a gender binary. This means a belief in two genders: male and female. However, some people do not fit this social structure. They do not identify as only male or only female. Rather, they may see themselves as both male and female, neither male nor female,

ADDING LABELS TO THE DICTIONARY

In 2016, the *Merriam-Webster Dictionary* added the terms *genderqueer* and *gender-fluid* to its unabridged version. It also changed outdated definitions for other terms, such as *nonbinary* and *gender identity*. Later that year, the *Oxford English Dictionary* also added the term *gender-fluid*.

People who did not agree with the terms lashed out against the *Merriam-Webster* and *Oxford English* dictionaries on social media. In response, the *Merriam-Webster* Twitter account tweeted, "People keep 1) saying they don't know what 'genderqueer' means then 2) asking why we added it to the dictionary."[3] Joel Baum, a senior director at Gender Spectrum, states that adding these words "helps to create [a] gender sensitive and inclusive environment for all children and teens." Baum added:

> There is literally a difficult convincing process that many non-binary people have to go through to 'prove' their existence or experiences are real. This [helps] the general public understand their experiences.[4]

or a combination of male and female. These individuals may refer to themselves as *genderqueer*, *nonbinary*, or *genderfluid*, among other labels.

Trans people may have trouble receiving equal treatment at work, in school, or in other aspects of daily life. According to trans man Brandon Studler, coming out during his senior year of high school was difficult. In an interview with *Teen Vogue* about his experiences starting college as an out trans man, he said, "I had to fight to get housing, I had to fight to get health care, to use the bathroom, to have my name changed on IDs. . . . It was really difficult existing in a space where I was the only [transgender student]." However, Studler believes that his persistence paid off for other trans students. He added, "Before I left, someone else came who was transgender, and everything for him was changed within a week [that] took me years to change. So I knew I had made a difference."[5]

TINDER BECOMES MORE INCLUSIVE

The popular dating app Tinder changed its software to be more inclusive. Until mid-2017, users could identify themselves as either *male* or *female* and either *heterosexual* or *homosexual*. After the update, users could choose from 37 descriptions or write their own gender-identity description. The update acknowledges users who are transgender. It also provides a means for users to reveal their gender to people they might date.

Two people with the same sexual orientation or gender identity may not have the same gender expression.

GENDER EXPRESSION

Gender expression is someone's external expression of their gender identity. Similar to sexuality and gender identity, gender expression is on a spectrum. The spectrum has *masculine* on one end and *feminine* on the other. Gender expression can be anywhere on that spectrum, regardless of a person's gender identity. For example, some trans women, such as actress Laverne Cox and reality TV star Caitlyn Jenner, dress in a feminine style. They wear dresses and skirts, jewelry, and makeup. Other trans women, such as activist Eli Erlick, dress in

The Genderbread Person v4

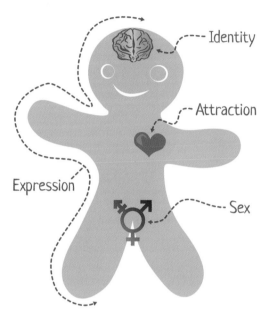

- - - Identity

- - - Attraction

Expression

- - - Sex

⊘ means a lack of what's on the right side

 Gender Identity
⊘ ——————————→ Woman-ness
⊘ ——————————→ Man-ness

 Gender Expression
⊘ ——————————→ Femininity
⊘ ——————————→ Masculinity

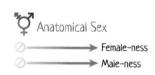 Anatomical Sex
⊘ ——————————→ Female-ness
⊘ ——————————→ Male-ness

Identity ≠ Expression ≠ Sex
Gender ≠ Sexual Orientation

Sex Assigned At Birth
☐ Female ☐ Intersex ☐ Male

 Sexually Attracted to...   and/or (a/o)
⊘ ——————————→ Women a/o Feminine a/o Female People
⊘ ——————————→ Men a/o Masculine a/o Male People

 Romantically Attracted to...
⊘ ——————————→ Women a/o Feminine a/o Female People
⊘ ——————————→ Men a/o Masculine a/o Male People

Gender identity, gender expression, and anatomical sex all exist on different spectrums.

a more masculine style. Erlick feels more comfortable dressing in what she calls a "dapper" style. In an Instagram post, she stated, "After transitioning, I felt the need to dress extra feminine to affirm my gender. Following years of confronting the brutal processes of gender conformity trans women are forced into, I now know my trans womanhood is valid no matter how I dress."[6]

Some people may name their gender expression as part of their identity. Some common labels include *butch*, *masc*, and *femme*. People who consider themselves butch or masc may feel more comfortable in masculine clothing. Lea DeLaria, who plays Big Boo in the television series *Orange Is the New Black*, always felt uncomfortable in

THE BUTCH-FEMME DYNAMIC

The labels *butch* and *femme* originated in lesbian communities in the mid-1900s. According to the website GLBTQ Archive, these labels were complex identities for lesbians. Butch lesbians took on more traditionally masculine roles in relationships, while femme lesbians took on more traditionally feminine roles. This was often referred to as the butch-femme dynamic. It was an important symbol of community for lesbians at the time.

According to an article on Autostraddle, a website for women in the LGBTQ community, the roles in a butch-femme relationship were fairly rigid in the 1950s. People who wanted to be in butch-butch or femme-femme relationships had to keep them secret. Later, these types of relationships became more common. While some people in the LGBTQ community still identify with the emotional aspects of the butch-femme dynamic, many people use these terms simply to refer to gender expression.

feminine clothes. She states that the first time she put on a well-fitted suit, "it was like putting on my own skin."[7]

People who consider themselves femme may feel more comfortable in feminine clothing. In an article for *Vice*, several people in the LGBTQ community discussed what the word *femme* meant to them. Maurice Tracy, who identifies as a "femme queer boi," says that *femme* is "both a celebration and a refiguring of femininity." Artemisia, who identifies as a "queer femme," says that the label "recognizes that I identify with aspects of femininity but don't identify with the heteronormative system" that devalues femininity.[8]

GENDER FLUIDITY

Some people identify as genderfluid. Their style of dress, the way they express themselves, and even the way they describe themselves moves between masculine and feminine.

Lee Luxion, who uses the pronouns *they* and *their*, is genderfluid. On any given day, Luxion might feel like a man, a woman, both, or neither. Luxion described their experience to CNN reporter Lauren Booker: "How I express it is usually how I dress, how I do my hair. But then my mannerisms change. The way I speak might change a little, too."

Someone who is genderfluid may or may not identify as transgender. And someone who expresses different gender presentations may not identify as genderfluid. As Luxion explained,

> Gender fluidity is much more than saying, "oh, I want to play up the [feminine] traits that I have" or that "I want to play up the masculine traits that I have." It's an actual physical, mental and, for me, emotional shift in how I interact with the world.[9]

Sassafras Lowrey agrees. Lowrey came out as genderqueer at the age of 17. Lowrey wrote about being nonbinary in an article for the *Huffington Post*: "Over the years my gender presentation has been fluid from: butch, to transgender man, to bearded lady, to queer femme. The only consistency in my gender identity over the years has been genderqueer, and my non-binary pronouns: ze/hir."[10]

DISCUSSION STARTERS

- What is your gender identity? How do you express it?
- What labels do you use to describe yourself?
- Why might labels be important to some people? Why do you think labels change over time?

Some societal norms, such as gendered colors, begin at birth.

FIGHTING
SOCIETAL NORMS

Societal norms are unspoken rules in society. They can be broad or specific. Some societal norms in the United States include making eye contact with someone while speaking and saying "bless you" when someone sneezes. Most of the time, norms exist so that society is more orderly. People follow societal norms so they can be accepted by their peers. But sometimes, societal norms are limiting.

Some societal norms tell people how to dress or act based on their gender. For example, men should not cry or wear dresses, and women should not be angry or wear suits. LGBTQ people often fight against these kinds of societal norms. For some people, their sexual and gender identities

Younger people, including those who are LGBTQ, have easier access to information than people of older generations did when they were young. According to 60-year-old Dot Brauer, genderqueer director of the University of Vermont LGBTQA Center, "All the information that came to me was filtered through some very sort of limited perspectives and limiting languages. So for example, if I was going to find out about gender, I was going to find out about it through health class in a curriculum that was set by the Board of Education."[1] The internet has changed that experience for millennials and younger generations, who can find information about gender expression and other LGBTQ topics online.

Lee Luxion, a genderfluid millennial, noted the importance of both the internet and famous genderfluid people. Luxion believes these factors have helped millennials feel safer expressing their gender identities. But Luxion also stated, "There shouldn't be a sense of what's normal or not. And [with] more representation of transgender or gender-fluid or non-binary individuals, the more likely it is that we are going to feel safe to also be that publicly."[2]

often go against the societal norms that favor heterosexual and cisgender people. However, even cisgender and heterosexual people are constrained by these norms.

HOW MANY LGBTQ PEOPLE ARE THERE?

Accurate statistics on the number of LGBTQ people in the United States are hard to obtain. Most statistics are estimates. The Williams Institute at the University of California, Los Angeles, School of Law studies sexual-orientation and gender-identity law and public policy. Gary Gates, an expert scholar at the institute, has said that the lack of accurate statistics is due to the surveys that are used. According to Gates, surveys have lacked consistency in defining *LGBTQ* and in their questions. For example, some surveys only include two or three labels for a person to choose from. They may also list *transgender* as a sexuality instead of a gender identity. These inaccuracies make it difficult for LGBTQ people to achieve accurate representation.

If the number of LGBTQ people is too low, for example, politicians may choose to ignore these constituents in favor of another group's interests.

Still, Gates has determined estimates of the LGBTQ population in the United States. Using 11 studies, Gates estimates that approximately nine million Americans are LGBTQ. Regarding the US population as a whole, Gates has theorized that approximately

HETEROSEXUALITY IN GENERATION Z

In 2018, the research company Ipsos MORI found that only 66 percent of people between the ages of 16 and 22 identified as "exclusively heterosexual." This number for Generation Z is lower than for previous generations, such as millennials (71 percent), Generation X (85 percent), and baby boomers (88 percent). Researchers believe that this shift is due to an awareness of different sexualities thanks to the amount of information on the internet. A person does not need to be either gay or straight. According to one of the report's authors, Hannah Shrimpton, "This generation . . . has grown up at a time when gender as a simple binary and fixed identity has been questioned much more widely—this is new, and will affect wider views of gender, sexuality and much broader aspects of identity."[3]

3.5 percent of people are lesbian, gay, or bisexual and
0.3 percent are transgender.[4]

LGBTQ people are a minority population. As a result,
lawmakers sometimes ignore bills related to LGBTQ people. This
means change can be slow. But it does not mean that activists
stop trying to make change. More and more organizations are
working to protect LGBTQ people—both youth and adults.

FINDING AN IDENTITY

While the LGBTQ community is varied, it is not necessarily all
inclusive. Some people in the LGBTQ community argue that
some people do not belong there. As a result, some people
who describe themselves as LGBTQ are struggling to be
acknowledged by others in the LGBTQ community.

One example of an excluded group is asexual people.
Heather Leah, editor in chief for the Candid Slice website, wrote
about being asexual in an article for the *Huffington Post*. Leah
described being asexual: "I don't really care what's between
a person's legs. After all, it's of no interest to me. I'm far more
interested in their soul, in our compatibility, and in whether or
not they'll play video games with me."

Leah wrote the *Huffington Post* article in response to a video
about identities included in the LGBTQ acronym. Some versions
of the acronym also include the letter *A* to include people who

are asexual. But the video said the *A* was for "ally." An ally is someone who supports the community but is not a member of it. The error made Leah feel erased again. She stated,

> *Once again, the . . . LGBT community has kicked my orientation out—as if it's not enough that the whole world kicks us out. Where do the Asexuals belong? . . . We should be recognized in the queer alphabet soup.*[5]

Asexual people protest to include the letter *A* for *asexual* in longer acronyms for the LGBTQ community.

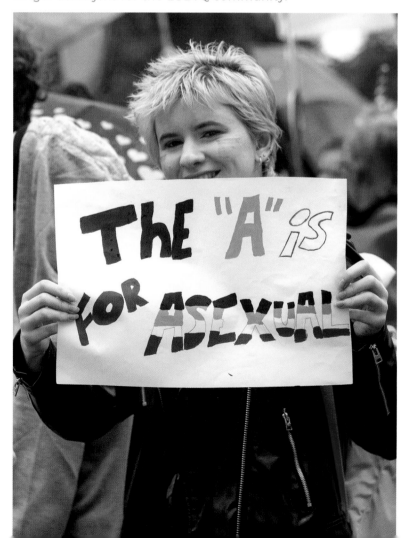

Bisexual people have also faced the challenge of erasure. An example is a bisexual woman who is dating a lesbian. People might assume the bisexual woman is a lesbian. They may refer to the couple as a lesbian couple. But the bisexual woman is not a lesbian. She dates men and women, so she corrects those who say "lesbian couple." The response she gets is dismissal. The people she corrects say the woman really is not bisexual or that being bisexual does not matter because she is in a relationship. Bisexual people who are dating someone of the opposite sex may also be excluded from LGBTQ spaces. In an article for *Cosmopolitan*, Charlotte Dingle wrote, "As a bi woman, being in a same-sex couple doesn't

GAY MARRIAGE, SAME-SEX MARRIAGE, AND MARRIAGE EQUALITY

The Supreme Court ruled on *Obergefell v. Hodges* in 2015. This guaranteed marriage equality across the United States. Many people referred to this as a ruling on gay marriage. However, advocates for marriage equality state that *gay marriage* is not the correct term. For example, two married bisexual men are not in a gay marriage just because they are two men. Thus, people began to use the term *same-sex marriage* to note marriages between two people of the same sex, regardless of their sexual orientation. After the ruling on *Obergefell v. Hodges*, many people began to use *marriage equality* to refer to the idea that two people, regardless of gender identity or sexual orientation, can get married in the United States. As of 2019, the GLAAD Media Reference Guide, a guide on LGBTQ terminology for people in the media, recommends using *marriage equality* or *marriage*. Other terms, the guide notes, "can suggest marriage for same-sex couples is somehow different than other marriages."[6]

Some stores separate clothing departments into boys' and girls' sections.

make us a lesbian, any more than being in an opposite-sex

couple makes us straight. Don't erase our identities and pasts."[7]

GENDERED PRODUCTS

Societal norms can make it difficult to express one's gender.

Consumers are faced with a variety of merchandise that is

marketed as being for men or for women. For example, some

stores have dolls in a toy aisle for girls and trucks in a toy aisle

for boys. Some companies market the same product in different colors or designs to appeal to females or males. Specifically, items for females are often pink or pastel, while those for males are often blue or dark, nonpastel colors. The Mars company sold M&M's in "Girls Rule" and "Boys Rule" mixes. The female version had candies in pink, green, and white. The male version was gray, blue, and red.

Such product gendering can be problematic. Lisa Wade, an associate professor of sociology at Occidental College, has noted issues with gendering products. First, these products reinforce the gender binary. Wade explained, "Outside of dating—for some of us—and making babies, gender really isn't that important in our real, actual daily lives."[8]

INTERSECTIONALITY AND GENDER EXPRESSION

Age, location, sex, socioeconomic class, race, gender, ability, and other identities come together to create a lens of intersectionality. The term *intersectionality* was coined by law professor Kimberlé Crenshaw to refer to the experience of being both black and a woman. People have different experiences based on how different parts of their identity come together. Dot Brauer has written about how intersectionality applies to gender expression in the LGBTQ community. Brauer offered an example, saying someone in the mid-Atlantic part of the United States might find Brauer "pretty masculine by the gender standards of femininity." In Vermont, however, where Brauer lives, the experience would be different because "the standards for gender and femininity are different. So, right here I would be seen not overly masculine and not overly feminine."[9]

Another issue with gendered products has to do with cost. These products are more expensive when designated for females. This is especially true of beauty, fashion, and health items. This disparity is called the "pink tax." The website *Vox* published the prices of some gendered products. One example was Schick razors. The package for men was $14.99. The package for women was $18.49. On average, razors marketed to women cost 11 percent more than those marketed to men. The difference in shampoo is even greater, with a 48 percent difference between women's shampoo and men's shampoo.[10]

The pink tax also includes items for children. One example is a scooter. The "boy's" model in red cost $24.99. The "girl's" model in pink cost $49.99. In general, toys marketed for girls cost 7 percent more than those marketed for boys. All totaled, the pink tax creates a difference of $1,351 per year between women and men.[11] These types of gender discrimination and stereotypes factor into LGBTQ discrimination.

DISCUSSION STARTERS

- What are some ways the pink tax affects you?
- What are some ways societal norms affect you?
- Do you believe there is a correct way to be a certain gender? Why or why not?

Coming out to loved ones can be an emotional conversation.

COMING OUT

For many people in the LGBTQ community, publicly acknowledging their identity is important. This is referred to as "coming out of the closet" or, more simply, as "coming out." According to historian George Chauncey, the metaphor of the closet came about in the 1960s. While its origin is unknown, Chauncey states that "it may have been used initially because many men who remained 'covert' thought of their homosexuality as a sort of 'skeleton in the closet.'"[1]

Sometimes coming out can be challenging or even dangerous. Not knowing how others may respond to one's sexuality or gender identity can cause worry, stress, and danger. However, coming out can also be a celebratory occasion of announcing one's identity to family and friends if they are accepting.

DECIDING WHETHER TO COME OUT

Coming out publicly about one's sexuality or gender identity is a personal decision. People come out at various ages, and

MICROAGGRESSIONS

Microaggressions are small statements or actions by people that hurt someone in a minority group. Over time, these microaggressions build up and become hard for a person to handle. All people are capable of committing microaggressions. Sometimes the person saying or doing the hurtful thing doesn't know it is hurtful. A cashier at a grocery store who calls a trans woman *sir* may not be trying to hurt the woman's feelings. Many people are taught to use *sir* and *ma'am* as a sign of respect. However, even accidentally misgendering someone still hurts them.

there is no timeline for when a person needs to come out or how long the process should take. Some people also decide never to come out for a variety of reasons, including personal safety and community acceptance. For example, some trans people try to blend in with cisgender people as though they are also cisgender. This is known in the trans community as being "stealth." There are many reasons why someone might choose to be stealth. For Beckham Loupe, a mechanic in Tennessee, he found it easier to be stealth on the job rather than answer personal questions from coworkers. However, Loupe says it is difficult to hear transphobic comments from coworkers and customers. He stated, "In those moments, I just want to stand up and say *hey, this is who I am*—but I would never ever do that."[2]

Other trans people have no intention of being perceived as cisgender. They may be outside the gender binary or feel uncomfortable being gendered. LGBTQ publication the

Advocate argued that trans people don't need to be perceived as cisgender; they need "society to broaden its concept of gender and expression and allow non-conformity to be an acceptable alternative to the male or female binary."[3]

Some people come out because they want to live openly as their preferred sexuality or gender identity and they want other people to know that status. For some people, not coming out feels dishonest. These people do not want to hide the genders of their romantic partners or their own gender expression.

Other people prefer not to come out. They may feel OK keeping their sexuality or gender identity private. They may not feel safe or supported enough to come out. Some trans people may also openly express their gender identity but remain private about the fact that they are trans. Many people are also out in some places but not out in others. For example, someone may be open about their sexuality with friends or family but not out at work or school. According to author Laila Ibrahim, "In my experience [coming out] is an ongoing part of life. Sometimes it's easy, and other times it makes my stomach flutter."[4]

The University of Washington Counseling Center offers guidance for students who are considering coming out to other people. The first is to select someone who is supportive as the first person to come out to, because that person can help the student cope with potential negative experiences.

LGBTQ youth can build a support system with their peers by coming out to supportive friends and community members.

Erica Ciszek, an assistant professor of communications at the University of Houston, studied LGBTQ youths' use of social media. Specifically, Ciszek studied social media outreach. She found that LGBTQ youth advocacy campaigns depicted more complex LGBTQ people than the pop-cultural portrayals of LGBTQ youth did. Ciszek also found that LGBTQ youth connected more with social media campaigns that highlighted other parts of who they are, such as race. She discussed the study with Cameron Wallace of *Out Smart*, an LGBTQ magazine in Houston, Texas:

> It showed the complexity of young people. Young people's narratives tend to be really flattened out. We try as adults, often, to come up with campaigns based on what we think they're about. . . . We can't just come up with one large mega-narrative that describes LGBTQ youth.[6]

The counseling center also advises students to prepare themselves for other people's initial reactions, which may be negative but may change over time. Some people need time to process the news. In addition, staying positive is important. The center states that people have the right to express themselves openly. They also mention that "in no case is another person's rejection evidence of your lack of worth or value."[5]

YOUTH COME OUT

According to Caitlin Ryan, director of the Family Acceptance Project at San Francisco State University, coming out during adolescence was historically uncommon. Most people came out as adults. The reason was fear. They did not want to be rejected or experience negative responses.

RELIGION AND BEING LGBTQ

Many people identify with a religion. But for people in the LGBTQ community, being religious may be difficult. Some religions believe and teach that being LGBTQ is abnormal or wrong. John R. Blosnich, a scientist at West Virginia University Injury Control Research Center, studied the relationship between religion and suicide in LGBTQ youth. Blosnich found that religion may keep heterosexual youth from attempting suicide. However, the opposite was true for LGBTQ youth. The greater the importance of religion for LGBTQ youth, the more likely they were to contemplate suicide.

LGBTQ youth may feel abandoned by their religion and church. This may cause them sadness and anger. In addition, some LGBTQ people may worry about their families' reactions if members are religious. Their families may not accept their gender identity or sexuality.

The Naming Project is a Christian organization that works to include LGBTQ individuals in the religion. Ross Murray, project director for the organization, believes this mission is important:

> *When religious communities are affirming and supportive of identity, including sexual orientation and gender identity, then the people within those communities are going to develop into much healthier and better-functioning individuals who understand themselves and how they relate to the rest of the world.*[7]

Numerous religious organizations are working to educate non-LGBTQ people. Some believe there is a different way to look at sacred texts that affirms and supports LGBTQ identities. This acceptance has a positive impact on LGBTQ youth.

Some religious leaders perform same-sex weddings, but others do not welcome same-sex couples into their places of worship.

Since the 1990s, the amount of LGBTQ resources has grown, particularly because of the internet. Young people have greater access to information on sexuality and gender identity. This can help people understand their identity at a younger age. It can also offer support and encouragement for people who may live in an unaccepting community. More recent developments also include school diversity groups and gay-straight alliances or gender-sexuality alliances, both referred to as GSAs.

Stephen Russell, a professor of family studies and human development at the University of Arizona, studied data gathered by the Family Acceptance Project. The project surveyed 245 Latino and white LGBTQ adults from ages 21 to 25. The respondents who had come out at school also reported having higher self-esteem and being more satisfied with life than the respondents who were not out in school. In addition, the respondents who were out at school indicated having less depression as young adults than the respondents who were not out at school.

Russell noted the links between coming out and a person's mental health. Mental health is more than simply the highs and lows one experiences or their reactions to daily events and particular situations. Rather, mental health has to do with a person's general thinking, feeling, and mood. Russell stated, "The thing that's encouraging is that we've found being out is good for you. This is clearly aligned with everything we

Social media sites such as Facebook can help young people learn about the LGBTQ community.

know about identity. Being able to be who we are is crucial to mental health."[8]

A 2017 survey done by the Human Rights Campaign (HRC) had similar findings. As the HRC explained in its report, "The youth in our survey who report that being out was a positive and affirming experience for them also report better outcomes in terms of their overall health and well-being."

Some respondents were clear in their self-confidence as people who identify as LGBTQ. One survey participant shared,

> I think being open with myself has made me prouder of my identity as a queer person. I know that. Regardless of what others think of my sexual orientation, I am able to love who I love and not be ashamed of it.[9]

THE IMPORTANCE OF ACCEPTANCE

LGBTQ youth are more likely to come out when they think they will be accepted. Errol Fields, pediatrician and adolescent medicine specialist at the Johns Hopkins University School of Medicine, discussed the importance of parental support on the hospital's website. He offered advice to parents, explaining that children's coming out to parents is often the toughest instance of coming out for someone in the LGBTQ community:

> Time and time again, we hear the same thing from patients: "Once my parents are behind me, I can handle anything else the world throws at me." You're their anchor, and your acceptance is key. In fact, research shows that LGBTQ adolescents who are supported by their families grow up to be happier and healthier adults.[10]

In 2017, the HRC partnered with the University of Connecticut to survey LGBTQ youth. More than 12,000 LGBTQ people ages 13 to 17 responded. They hailed from all 50 states and Washington, DC. Of those surveyed, 24 percent reported they can "definitely" be their true LGBTQ selves at home. In contrast, 67 percent of respondents reported hearing their families speak negatively about LGBTQ people. One respondent explained, "Any resurgence of the topic of queer people typically results in attacks on my identity."[11]

Some people internalize the negative messages and lack of acceptance from society, focusing the messages inward on themselves. This can erode a person's self-esteem. As the Gay Therapy Center explained on its website, "The impact of growing up and living in a family and world that marginalizes gay people is profound. Many of us were flooded with shame at a young age when we were not equipped to deal with it."[12]

NATIONAL COMING OUT DAY

October 11 is National Coming Out Day. This is the anniversary of the March on Washington for Lesbian and Gay Rights in 1987. Marchers protested in favor of LGBTQ rights. They also marched to force the government to acknowledge the acquired immunodeficiency syndrome (AIDS) crisis in the United States.

National Coming Out Day is celebrated by many youth in the LGBTQ community. The Trevor Project, a nonprofit organization that has a suicide hotline and crisis prevention counselors for LGBTQ youth, speaks with many people around National Coming Out Day. According to Trevor Project chief executive officer (CEO) Amit Paley, "We want to make sure that young people aren't coming out just because they feel pressured to do so by a holiday, but are doing so because they themselves have made the choice best for them."[13]

In addition, such internalization may not go away entirely. Campus Pride, a nonprofit organization focused on developing a safe school environment for LGBTQ college students, discusses healing from oppression on its website: "Because of the strength of early socialization and continued exposure to anti-LGBTQ attitudes, internalized oppression can remain a factor in the LGBTQ students' adjustment throughout college."[14]

Several factors positively influence the mental health of LGBTQ youth. For transgender youth, one of those factors is to socially or physically transition. This may include changing their physical appearance or beginning hormone therapy or hormone replacement therapy (HRT). These acts are

BEING OUTED

Actress Samira Wiley of *Orange Is the New Black* was outed by one of her cast members. This means that the cast member told others that Wiley was a lesbian before Wiley was ready to tell other people. Wiley says that she cried when she saw her sexuality mentioned in a magazine. She adds that coming out was "something somebody took from me."[15]

Outing someone can be very dangerous. They may not be in a safe community or may not be ready to come out. According to Stonewall, an LGBTQ organization in the United Kingdom, "Publicly outing someone robs that person of the chance to define who they are in their own terms."[16] Many celebrities in the LGBTQ community are outed before they have a chance to come out of the closet on their own terms. Some celebrities who have been outed include Lee Pace, Carrie Brownstein, and Neil Patrick Harris. Stonewall argues that while having LGBTQ role models is important, this should not come at the cost of an individual person's safety or well-being.

important for trans children to begin to live as their true selves. Transitioning lowers feelings of depression. A lower rate of depression correlates to lower use of drugs and alcohol.

Social support may also help with self-esteem. Researchers in Texas and the Netherlands studied a group of LGBTQ individuals ages 13 to 20 who took part in Hatch Youth, a youth group. Those who participated for more than one month experienced more social support than individuals who participated for less than one month. The researchers found that having more social support was linked to having less depression, more self-esteem, and better coping skills.[17]

PARENTAL SUPPORT

Parents can help their LGBTQ children in many ways. Talking is important. Connecting and communicating regularly will help when more significant topics or issues arise, such as dating and sex. Understanding what it means to be LGBTQ is also important. Renata Sanders, a doctor at Johns Hopkins, noted that parents often have misunderstandings or wrong information about sexual orientation and gender identity. It is important that parents understand that children in the LGBTQ community are not simply going through a phase, even though someone's gender identity or sexual orientation may change over time.

Parental support of gender and sexuality plays a large role in a teen's mental health.

Parents can also help their LGBTQ children by being involved in the community. This includes communicating with teachers regularly, keeping an eye out for bullying, and advocating for GSAs. Sanders noted the power of parents when it comes to their children's schools: "Parents forget that they have a huge voice in the school system. You do have power. If there's a problem and the school isn't taking your concerns seriously, go to the principal or even the school board."[18]

Having healthy relationships is important for youth. But dating can be a challenging topic for many parents. However, parental acceptance of a child's partner can positively affect that child's mental health. Fields said, "By encouraging your kid to date in a way that's healthy and age-appropriate, you send a powerful message: LGBTQ relationships are normal, and there's nothing to hide or be ashamed of."[19]

DISCUSSION STARTERS

- In what ways are you open about your sexuality and gender identity? What things do you keep private?

- Aside from simply telling others one's gender or sexual identity, what are some other ways people choose to come out?

- Acceptance is key for positive mental health. What are some steps you can take to create a more accepting space in your school or community?

THE SCHOOL EXPERIENCE

The school experience varies greatly from person to person, from a time of fun and friendship, to one of sadness and solitude. The school experience also varies for LGBTQ youth. Schools can provide safety and affirmation for LGBTQ youth who may not receive the same validation at home. But schools are also the places where LGBTQ youth are likely to experience harassment from peers and faculty. Without the right supports and school policies, LGBTQ youth are more likely to drop out than their non-LGBTQ peers.

SAFETY AND SUPPORT

Most LGBTQ youth struggle with feeling safe and supported at school. In its 2018 LGBTQ Youth Report, the HRC reported that only 26 percent of respondents to its 2017 survey felt safe all the time while

TRANSGENDER ATHLETES

In June 2018, two female athletes faced controversy. Terry Miller and Andraya Yearwood ran track for their Connecticut high schools. Both have placed in state high school tournaments. They are also transgender, which has caused some parents and students to question school policy regarding transgender athletes. Some people believe that trans girl athletes have an unfair advantage over cis girl athletes. Some parents wanted transgender athletes to take hormones corresponding with their gender identity. The Connecticut Interscholastic Athletic Conference allows transgender athletes to play on the sports team that aligns with their gender identity. It does not require the athletes to take hormones.

Many barriers exist for trans athletes. For example, some trans girls are not allowed to play on a girls' sports team because people believe that they are just boys who want a competitive advantage. Some trans boys are forced to play on the girls' sports team due to rules about playing on the team that corresponds with the sex they were assigned at birth. However, then people sometimes argue that these boys, who may be undergoing hormone replacement therapy (HRT), have an unfair advantage over their female competitors.

in their classes. And only 5 percent of LGBTQ students felt supported by all of their teachers and school staff.[1]

Bullying is a large issue for LGBTQ youth. According to the report, 70 percent of LGBTQ respondents reported being bullied at school because of their sexual orientation. Forty-three percent had experienced bullying at school in the last year. Bullying goes beyond fellow students. Teachers and staff can also pick on LGBTQ students. One survey participant described bullying experiences that had happened at school:

When I asked the principal to help my situation, he laughed at me and told me I was overreacting. I've also had teachers look me in my eyes and tell me they do not support same-sex marriage and transgender people, so I find it extremely hard to trust the adults at my school because they more than likely share the same opinions.[2]

The unaccepting environment many LGBTQ students experience at school can have negative effects. In 2016, the Gay, Lesbian, and Straight Education Network (GLSEN) reported that middle and high school students who identify as LGBTQ tend to have poorer grades, poorer attendance, and poorer graduation rates. Emily Greytak, GLSEN's director of research, said of her findings, "We see that LGBT youth are being deprived of an equal education based on these hostile school environments."[3]

PROM

One extracurricular activity many high school students enjoy is prom. For some LGBTQ students, though, prom results in another instance of exclusion. In February 2018, 17-year-old Janizia Ross asked her girlfriend to prom. She arranged the prom proposal, or "promposal," during a talent show at their public Alabama school, Alexandria High School. The school's principal gave Ross an in-school suspension, reportedly for violating a school rule that prohibits promposals at school events. Ross's mother told a local news station that the principal announced to students via the public address system that their school is a "Christian school" and apologized to those who were offended by the same-sex promposal.[4]

SCHOOL SUPPORT FOR TRANS STUDENTS

According to a 2017 survey by the US Centers for Disease Control, almost 2 percent of high schoolers identify as trans.[5] While some trans students have a difficult time in school, other students report that their school experience has been positive. In 2016, trans girl Violet Bezelik, then 14 years old, discussed her high school experience in an interview with the National Education Association. Bezelik was homeschooled in eighth grade in order to make her social transition, including a legal name change, easier.

On her first day of high school, Bezelik noted that her teachers used her correct name and pronouns, and other teachers checked to make sure that she wasn't being harassed by other students. Bezelik said that this support "makes me feel a whole lot better about being a transgender teenager. When I have people who care, keep me safe, and defend me . . . it definitely makes me feel like I can take on the world." Bezelik's father agreed that affirming and respectful teachers made a huge difference to the school experience. He added, "Using the right name and pronouns can give so much validation to kids, who may not get it at home. It could save their lives."[6]

McKinley High School in Buffalo, New York, had a history of not allowing same-sex couples at the school's dances. When students bought couples tickets for a dance, they had to provide the names of their dates. When the date was the same sex as the student, the school would not allow them to buy tickets. Junior Byshop Elliott filed a lawsuit in 2017. Shortly after, the school changed its policy about same-sex couples at school dances.

Other students have taken a different approach. In April 2018, a group of LGBTQ teens in West Virginia organized the Rainbow Formal. It was the state's first LGBTQ youth dance. Students from at least ten counties attended the event. Sam

Green, a junior who is transgender, was one of the organizers. Green talked about the importance of the dance with NBC News:

> The goal is that one day we don't need to have this ... students
> won't have to worry about going to school or going to dances
> or anything like that and having to worry ... if [it's] a same-sex
> relationship or being transgender and anybody thinking poorly
> of that.[7]

BuzzFeed hosted a Queer Prom in 2017. Openly gay singer Adam Lambert, *right*, crowned some of the attendees who could not go to prom at their own schools.

One parent attended the dance. Tiffany was there to support Jazmine, her pansexual daughter. Tiffany did Jazmine's hair and lent her a pair of red high heels. Tiffany was clear about supporting her daughter, saying, "There's nowhere I would be other than here today, because whether she's going to Rainbow Formal or a traditional prom—or marrying a man or marrying a woman or whatever—I'm going to be there."[8]

MAKING SCHOOLS BETTER

One way LGBTQ students have been supported in the fight against bullying is in legislation. Lawmakers in 19 states and Washington, DC, have passed antibullying laws. These laws were designed to protect LGBTQ students from students, teachers, and school staff.

At the school level, having safe spaces is important. A simple sticker designating a classroom as safe can really make

Accommodations such as gender-neutral restrooms can help LGBTQ students feel safe in the school environment.

a difference for LGBTQ students. Queen Cornish, who identifies

as LGBTQ, was a sophomore at Mount Pleasant High School

in Wilmington, Delaware, in 2016. Queen was the subject

of name-calling and gossip and had the painful experience

of someone telling her she was an "abomination." Queen

discussed feeling safe in school with the *Atlantic* magazine:

"A lot of teachers have 'safe space' stickers on their doors. Those little signs are great because they let you know that the teacher is going to respect your identity."[9]

Training teachers is another critical step in making schools better for LGBTQ students. GLSEN's 2016 report includes responses from teachers who took part in the survey. Half of the teachers said they had made no efforts to support LGBTQ students attending their schools. In contrast, 83 percent of the teachers said they thought they had a responsibility to make sure LGBTQ students had a safe environment for learning.[10] Emily Greytak thinks the difference between the teachers' feeling of duty toward LGBTQ students and not acting on it may be resolved with training. Training includes educating teachers about LGBTQ-specific issues. Trainers can help teachers learn how to bring up LGBTQ topics in class. Training also gives teachers the tools to be supportive when LGBTQ-identified students come to them for help.

CREATING AN INCLUSIVE CLIMATE

One factor that has had a positive result on LGBTQ students' school experience is having a GSA. GSAs are for people who identify as LGBTQ, who are wondering if they are LGBTQ, who have friends or family members who identify as LGBTQ, or who simply want to support the LGBTQ community. A GSA is a student organization where students can come together

SEX EDUCATION

One area of school where LGBTQ students are often overlooked is sex education. Inclusive sex education has led to decreased rates in unprotected sex, teen pregnancy, and the occurrence of sexually transmitted infections. However, many students have not received LGBTQ-focused sex education. Most students received no sex education in school, or the sex education is about heterosexual cisgender relationships. Additionally, students do not receive comprehensive information about intersex people or asexuality. As a result, LGBTQ youth may turn to friends, classmates, and the internet for information. That information may be misinformed or outdated. In addition to leaving students uninformed, the lack of LGBTQ sex education factors into school environments that aren't inclusive.

Different elements have contributed to the lack of sex education focused on LGBTQ topics. For example, one element is laws about sex education. In some states, schools have "Don't Say Gay" policies, where teachers are prohibited from discussing pro-LGBTQ material.

to meet and discuss openly and honestly without fear of rejection or attack. In addition to providing a safe, supportive environment for members, GSAs also provide education about LGBTQ issues. GLSEN has a variety of material for GSAs. Its free resources include lessons and discussion guides, as well as GSA-specific guidance, such as finding a GSA faculty adviser. GSAs can also register their group at GLSEN's website and join the network of more than 6,500 GSAs that exist in the United States.

GSAs educate others by promoting LGBTQ events such as Ally Week, the Transgender Day of Visibility (TDOV), and Day of Silence. Ally Week is a time for allies of the LGBTQ community

Some schools ban books, such as *And Tango Makes Three*, that reference same-sex couples positively. Other schools include LGBTQ-positive books in their curriculums.

to show their support. TDOV is March 31. It is meant to help trans people feel accepted as well as provide information and resources for all people. Day of Silence, held in April, brings attention to the bullying and harassment of LGBTQ people. Those who choose to participate take a vow of silence while they are in school that day. Instead of talking, they pass out cards that explain their silence.

One student in the HRC's 2017 survey shared an example of how the GSA helped, saying it gave all the school's teachers safe space stickers and most of the teachers used them. That was important for the LGBTQ student, who said about the stickers being on display, "I know that I won't be judged for talking about my identity." Another respondent talked about being president of the GSA and the importance of that role: "I . . . am looked to as a role model for younger students, so I try to talk to adults frequently about my sexual orientation and experience."[11] GSA student leaders often take on activist roles within their schools. Groups hold events and campaigns to raise awareness and make changes to the school climate.

IMPROVING THE SCHOOL EXPERIENCE

In addition to designating safe spaces and providing a GSA, schools can take other steps to improve the school experience for LGBTQ students. One is by including LGBTQ topics in the curriculum.

GLSEN reported that covering LGBTQ history and issues may help LGBTQ students. Positive representations reduce intolerance and prejudice. LGBTQ students see firsthand that

Supportive teachers and role models help LGBTQ youth have better outcomes in school.

other LGBTQ people exist in the world. This promotes feelings of self-acceptance and pride.

Michael Sadowski, an expert in adolescent identity development, has spoken with countless LGBTQ youth about their experiences. Sadowski has learned from LGBTQ students how having just one teacher they can rely on and be able to talk to can really affect their school experience and how the students feel about themselves. This includes both teachers in the LGBTQ community and teachers who are allies. But teachers in the LGBTQ community would understand students' experiences. Sadowski said in an interview with National Public Radio (NPR), "The best school leaders think a lot about [diversity] when they hire staff. They should also think about making sure LGBTQ students have positive role models at school."[12]

Making the school experience better for students will require a multifaceted approach. The results of changes, when implemented, could make a world of difference in classrooms, in halls, on courts and fields, and beyond.

DISCUSSION STARTERS

- How safe do you think your school is for LGBTQ students? Explain your answer.

- Besides putting up posters and safe space stickers, what are some other actions teachers and school staff can take to show their support of LGBTQ students?

- What do you think sex education curriculum should include?

6

LGBTQ youth can meet chosen families and role models through school or community groups.

FINDING FAMILY
AND ROLE MODELS

Feeling alone and lonely is a common human experience. And it can be emotionally painful. In 2009, the University of California, Davis, Center for Reducing Health Disparities (CRHD) published a report about LGBTQ youth and mental health. The report was the result of discussions with LGBTQ youth about their mental health needs. Isolation was a concern for the youth, and it factored into their mental health. Specifically, the youth talked about feeling isolated by a variety of groups, including family, peers, and social organizations, such as churches.

LGBTQ individuals face challenges in all areas of life. One factor that can have a strong positive effect on an LGBTQ person is family. However, many LGBTQ people experience a lack of family acceptance. As a result, they are left to create a found or chosen family. Role models also shine a light in what

DRAG BALLS AND BALL CULTURE

Many LGBTQ people find a sense of community at drag balls. At these events, participants compete against each other in drag, participating in various categories. These may include best dressed or business executive. Realness is a common category in which judges rate participants on their skill at appearing as heterosexual females or males.

Ball culture developed in the 1920s in New York City and the surrounding area. Initially, it was only white men having drag fashion shows. Black people sometimes participated, but the culture was racist and required them to make their faces appear lighter. The black ball culture formed in the 1960s. In the 1970s, drag balls increased in number and variety. They also became places for LGBTQ people of color to express themselves safely. Ball culture has hit the mainstream, in part because of the documentary *Paris Is Burning* and the success of drag queen RuPaul. The reality show *RuPaul's Drag Race*, a drag competition, aired on premium cable network Logo starting in 2009. As its audience grew, the show moved to VH1 in 2017.

can seem like a bleak world. Together, chosen families and role models can provide LGBTQ youth with hope.

CHOSEN FAMILY

Many people struggle with acceptance from their families. This is especially true for countless people who identify as LGBTQ. In November 2017, *Vice* reported that 39 percent of LGBTQ adults have suffered rejection from their families. In addition, 40 percent of homeless youth identify as LGBTQ, meaning thousands of LGBTQ youth are not living with and being supported by their families.[1] For these LGBTQ people, family is sorely lacking. They are missing the love and support that

LGBTQ youth may turn to friends and peers for support if their families do not approve of their gender identity or sexual orientation.

their families are expected to provide. But that does not mean these—or any other—queer individuals are without a family. Many LGBTQ people have a found or chosen family.

As the name suggests, the members of this family are found or chosen. In other words, an LGBTQ person chooses their family, creating it from close, loving, supportive people they trust. Jacob Tobia, a contributor to NBC Out, the LGBTQ section of NBC News's website, spoke about chosen families in November 2016. Tobia described chosen families as "a concept that's become fundamental to how many LGBTQ folks gain support, love, and affirmation."[2]

Tobia noted other important features of chosen families. Family members can be mentors, and they can provide information about LGBTQ culture and history. In addition, the size of one's chosen family is unlimited. Tobia described their

Some chosen families come together because they have similar interests or goals.

chosen family: "I, for one, have seven sisters, three moms, two grandmothers, and counting."[3]

More than 60 percent of LGBTQ people in the baby boomer generation have a chosen family.[4] This family is not necessarily biological or legal, and it may include straight and queer people alike. Some chosen families form through a shared interest. For example, the chosen family My Parade is a group of five LGBTQ people of color who live in Seattle, Washington. And the Carnival Kings is a group of 30 drag kings in New Orleans, Louisiana. Chosen families also do not necessarily live together. But in addition to offering love, kindness, and support, they may offer food and a place to sleep.

Some US cities recognize the importance of chosen families

COMMUNITIES ON SOCIAL MEDIA

Many LGBTQ people find support on social media sites. These users can find communities to view photos, read stories, and learn about LGBTQ events—or to post about any or all of these. For some users, Twitter and other sites are lifelines, connecting them to people who give them positivity and validation. Social media is particularly important for some users because it is the only place where they are out. A bisexual Twitter user named Beverly spoke about her experience with journalist John Paul Brammer. Beverly had not come out to her family, but she was out on Twitter. She said, "I get to be my truest self on here and with my friends, and that's what matters the most to me."[5] For some people, social media has helped them better understand themselves and find courage when their real-life environments may not have been as supportive.

in legislation. For example, workers in Los Angeles, California, and New York, New York, can use their paid time off to take care of members of their chosen family. The nonprofit organization A Better Balance works to create equality and increase choices for workers regarding caring for their families without losing their income or jobs. In its 2018 year-end report about chosen families, the organization wrote, "Due to the successes in 2018 and recent years, an estimated 20 million workers in the U.S. now have the legal right to use paid sick time to care for extended and chosen family."[6]

GLAAD

One of several organizations that support and advocate for LGBTQ people is GLAAD. Formed in 1985 and previously known as the Gay and Lesbian Alliance against Defamation, GLAAD changed its name in 2013 to indicate its inclusion of all LGBTQ people. According to its website, "GLAAD works through entertainment, news, and digital media to share stories from the LGBTQ community that accelerate acceptance."[7] GLAAD does this through different avenues. One is working with people who create movies and television shows to develop LGBTQ characters who are realistic, including in their diversity. Another involves working with news organizations on developing accurate, positive LGBTQ stories.

FINDING ROLE MODELS IN THE MEDIA

In addition to one's chosen family, seeing strong LGBTQ characters on television can provide hope and encouragement. But finding LGBTQ representation on TV can

Dominique Jackson, a trans woman actress, plays Elektra Abundance in *Pose*.

be difficult. GLAAD studies LGBTQ characters on cable TV and streaming services. In 2015, GLAAD's annual *Where We Are on TV* report concluded that shows lacked diversity. LGBTQ characters were lacking in number—broadcast TV had no transgender characters—and in racial diversity. That is, LGBTQ characters were predominately white. GLAAD CEO and president Sarah Kate Ellis discussed the importance of this dual diversity: "Each of us lives at the intersection of many identities and it's important that television characters reflect the full diversity of the LGBT community."[8]

Two years later, GLAAD's report for the 2017–2018 season showed improvement. For the most part, the number of recurring LGBTQ characters increased. Of note, 17 were transgender, including nine trans women, four trans men, and four nonbinary people. It was the first time GLAAD had found nonbinary characters. That report reflected another first: two asexual characters.[9] However, the study found racial diversity was still an issue.

LGBTQ representation in the media is improving thanks to programs such as *Pose* and *Queer Eye*. *Pose* is an FX series that premiered in June 2018. Set in 1980s New York City, the program showcases ball culture. Ball culture is part of the black and Latinx LGBTQ subculture. *Pose* contrasts ball culture with other cultures, such as the lives of the rich and those in the literary world. In addition to teaching about ball culture and some LGBTQ history, the series also highlights chosen families and the critical purpose they serve.

Another important feature of *Pose* is its cast. Many actors in *Pose* are trans people of color. According to *Variety*, "The show features the largest cast of transgender actors in series regular roles ever, as well as the largest recurring cast of LGBTQ actors ever for a scripted series."[10] Many people behind the scenes

Queer Eye won three Emmys in 2018.

are also trans, including writers and producers Janet Mock and
Our Lady J.

The program *Queer Eye* presents LGBTQ people in real life.
In this reality series, five gay men—the Fab Five—with different
talents work to help others by giving them makeovers and
advice. The Fab Five's work is important in different ways. In
addition to making over and guiding participants, the hosts
work with people who might not otherwise meet someone
who identifies as LGBTQ. Eva Reign wrote about the importance
of *Queer Eye* and the Fab Five to the show's participants:
"On *Queer Eye*, Americans who are seldom exposed to queer
folk . . . are challenged to open their hearts and allow a group
of queer men [to] help them better themselves in a variety of
ways, from how they dress to how they eat."[11]

Reign also feels connected to the show in a personal way. Reign is an African American trans woman who found great support from her cisgender gay friends as she transitioned. Reign explained how the show resonates with her experience with her chosen family: "When queer people come together, they can offer a familial sense of comfort we're often denied, both within our own families and on a broader social scale."[12]

TYLER OAKLEY'S CHOSEN FAMILY

In 2007, Tyler Oakley started a YouTube channel. He was 18 years old and a college freshman. His first video was a tour of his dorm room. He posted the video for his friends from high school who were attending other colleges. Eventually, Oakley became a YouTube sensation, with millions of subscribers and hundreds of millions of views. In 2017, he launched *Chosen Family*, an eight-part series, to share stories about resilience and present parts of LGBTQ history that are not well known. Topics included coming out, being an LGBTQ refugee, and the Stonewall riots, which were part of the fight for LGBTQ rights.

This positivity extends to the internet. Social media sites offer platforms for LGBTQ people to connect and form communities, regardless of whether they are out or whether they post about themselves. Sites such as YouTube have a wealth of LGBTQ content. Tyler Oakley, who identifies as gay, is a YouTube celebrity, with more than seven million subscribers. He also has more than six million Twitter followers, is a published author, and has used his YouTube popularity to become an activist. According to

Out magazine, Oakley is "one of the most widely-viewed queer voices on the Internet."[13] Oakley takes advantage of YouTube to discuss LGBTQ topics, including bullying and safe sex. He posts humorous videos too. Oakley's YouTube channel offers LGBTQ youth a place to learn, laugh, relate, and find strength.

DISCUSSION STARTERS

- How might a chosen family be helpful to someone who identifies as LGBTQ?

- Do you think portraying more LGBTQ people in the media is important? Why or why not?

- How do you use social media to find or share information? How does social media help shape your identities? What are some of the limitations of social media?

LGBTQ youth face discrimination in many ways, including how often they are stopped and arrested by law enforcement.

THE CHALLENGES OF DISCRIMINATION

People who identify as LGBTQ face a variety of issues because of that identity. An important challenge is discrimination. It can affect an individual in multiple important ways. Young people who identify as LGBTQ have experienced unequal treatment in the health-care and justice systems, as well as elsewhere in society, because of how they identify.

HEALTH CARE

One area where discrimination can mean the difference between life and death is health care. In 2015, more than two dozen states did not have anti-LGBTQ discrimination laws. That year, Kyler Prescott, a transgender boy, died from suicide. Fourteen-year-old Prescott had suicidal thoughts and had hurt himself. Katharine Prescott took her son to Rady Children's

Hospital in San Diego, California, for a 72-hour stay. She made clear that the staff should treat her son as a male. The staff treated Prescott as a girl. Prescott's mom tried to make them stop. The hospital released Prescott after only 24 hours even though the staff acknowledged that Prescott's mental health issues were serious. Prescott killed himself five weeks later.

The treatment Prescott received was not unusual. A 2017 survey by the College of American Pathologists found that LGBTQ patients experience a variety of discrimination by health-care professionals. Nine percent of people surveyed reported abusive or harsh language during treatment,

UNEQUAL CARE

Seeking care can be critical for someone dealing with mental health issues. Finding a therapist with whom one feels comfortable, understood, and supported can provide the positive relationship and environment an LGBTQ person might otherwise lack. But mental health treatment has a less-than-supportive history for people who identify as LGBTQ. In the 1950s and 1960s, many psychiatrists treated homosexuality and bisexuality as mental illnesses. They tried to cure these patients' sexuality. Others tried to cure trans people of their gender identities.

A big change came in the 1980s when the American Psychiatric Association stopped classifying being gay or lesbian as a mental illness. Another change was adding gender dysphoria to the *Diagnostic and Statistical Manual of Mental Disorders* (*DSM*). Dysphoria is the stress that can result when a person has a gender identity that does not match the sex they were assigned at birth. Previously, being transgender was in the *DSM* as gender identity disorder. This means that being transgender was considered the issue that needed to be treated. Today, most doctors treat the anxiety and depression associated with dysphoria.

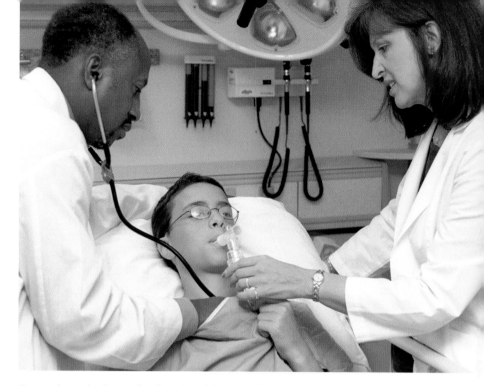

Some hospitals and other health-care facilities may not know how to treat LGBTQ patients. They may also discriminate against trans patients.

and 8 percent had a medical professional refuse to see them. Transgender people reported having these types of experiences more often. Twenty-one percent of transgender respondents had experienced abusive or harsh treatment, and 29 percent had a medical professional refuse to see them.[1] Other discrimination included health-care personnel intentionally calling the person by the wrong name or gender and unwanted physical contact.

LICENSE TO DISCRIMINATE

Some discrimination LGBTQ individuals face is made possible by laws. One example is in health care. Section 1557 of the Affordable Care Act, commonly known as Obamacare, addresses discrimination and makes discrimination based on gender identity a form of sex discrimination and therefore unlawful. In May 2017, the US Department of Health and Human Services (HHS) took steps to remove that discrimination rule.

The Human Rights Watch (HRW), an international, nonprofit, human rights organization, reported on this and other federal changes in its July 2018 report on LGBTQ discrimination in US health care. According to the report, in April 2018, the HHS officially proposed a rule to undo the Obamacare regulations designed to help transgender individuals receive health care. The federal agency also took steps to allow health-care providers to deny health care based on the providers' religious beliefs. This included creating a new department, the Office of Civil Rights, to deal with claims by health-care workers who express concerns about giving care to patients because of the worker's religious beliefs. According to the HRW report, "Together, these developments threaten to exacerbate the barriers to care that LGBT people already encounter, and give insurers and providers who would deny services to LGBT people, women, and others a license to discriminate against them."[2] The HRW is concerned about the effects of such policy changes on LGBTQ individuals and others who could suffer as a result. For example, people who need or want birth control

LGBTQ people who are also racial minorities face more discrimination than their LGBTQ peers who are white.

could be denied care. The organization encouraged lawmakers at all levels to enact legislation that limits discrimination.

GENDER, SEXUALITY, AND RACE

For many LGBTQ youth of color, racism is part of everyday existence. Being LGBTQ and a racial minority results in more discrimination for that individual than for peers who are heterosexual or white and LGBTQ. This can lead to negative effects on a person's mental health.

Eighty percent of LGBTQ youth of color who took part in the HRC's 2017 survey reported personally experiencing racism, and 20 percent said they think about racism daily. LGBTQ youth of color who discussed mental health needs with the CRHD also expressed having experienced homophobia, racism, and discrimination. One respondent noted negative representation in the media:

> Look at any gay magazine. Most of the people you see in our community . . . don't look like this room. They're not a rainbow. They're all white people. And like the best thing to be in the gay community is a gay, white male, you know. And it's like if you're anything else . . . it's not cool.[3]

Racial discrimination occurs in other areas as well. For example, LGBTQ youth who are black or Hispanic are more likely than white LGBTQ youth to become homeless. And people of color in the LGBTQ community experience discrimination twice as often as their white counterparts when applying for a job.

Racial discrimination also includes LGBTQ individuals' interactions with law enforcement. While police officers stop LGBTQ youth more often than they stop non-LGBTQ youth, they stop LGBTQ youth of color more often than they stop their LGBTQ peers who are white. For example, a 2014 survey conducted by BreakOUT! and the National Council on Crime & Delinquency found that police officers in New Orleans, Louisiana, stopped 33 percent of white LGBTQ youth and 87 percent of LGBTQ youth of color.[4]

Dealing with the compounded discrimination created by being LGBTQ and a person of color can be difficult, if not overwhelming. That makes having social and professional support crucial. However, in general, such support is lacking. Youth of color reported to the CRHD that they lacked resources, particularly LGBTQ role models and therapists of color.

HOMELESSNESS

Homelessness is another problem that affects the physical and mental health of LGBTQ youth. In November 2017, the University of Chicago research and policy center Chapin Hall released its report about youth homelessness in the United States. Researchers found that while less than 10 percent of children in the United States are in the LGBTQ community, more than 40 percent of children experiencing homelessness are in the LGBTQ community.[5]

Many LGBTQ youth who are homeless were forced out of their homes by their parents

THE FOSTER SYSTEM

Research estimates that approximately 400,000 LGBTQ youth are in the foster system in the United States. LGBTQ youth are overrepresented in the foster system. Nonheterosexual youth account for nearly 14 percent of foster children. Noncisgender youth make up 5.6 percent of the foster population but only 2.2 percent of the national population.[6]

LGBTQ youth face discrimination in the foster system. However, youth who are placed in homes with LGBTQ-identified foster parents often get much-needed affirmation. Many LGBTQ youth arrive in foster care because their parents rejected them. Finding a foster family that accepts them helps LGBTQ foster youth develop more positive self-esteem.

Trans teens may have a more difficult time when experiencing homelessness than cis teens.

or guardians. Some were in the foster care system and aged out without adequate support. Others ran away from home if their parents and family were not supportive of their gender identity or sexuality. Approximately 25 percent of homeless LGBTQ youth first experienced homelessness before they were 16. According to the National Coalition for the Homeless, people who identify as LGBTQ often struggle to find shelters that will accept them and respect them as LGBTQ individuals. The organization notes that finding shelter can be even more challenging for transgender individuals, stating on its website,

"Transgender people are particularly at physical risk due to a lack of acceptance and are often turned away from shelters."[7]

Being homeless can have multiple adverse effects on youth. According to the True Colors Fund, which works to end homelessness among LGBTQ youth, LGBTQ youth experiencing homelessness have an increased risk for "victimization, unsafe sexual practices, and mental health issues" than do other youth experiencing homelessness.[8]

According to the 2015 US Transgender Survey, one in three transgender people experiences homelessness at some point in their life.[9] Trans people experiencing homelessness have few resources. Shelters are often divided by gender. Many trans people are put in rooms with people based on the sex they were assigned at birth. Because of this, trans people are less likely to go to shelters. Additionally, some shelters turn away trans children. But those trans children may have run away from families that did not accept them. This leaves trans youth with few options for housing.

THE JUVENILE JUSTICE SYSTEM

Chapin Hall stated that the number of LGBTQ people experiencing homelessness may relate to the disproportionate LGBTQ representation in the US juvenile justice system. In 2016, the Center for American Progress and the Movement

Transgender youth who are incarcerated may have a hard time accessing resources related to transitioning or mental health.

Advancement Project published a report on LGBTQ youth in the juvenile justice system. According to the report, 7 to 9 percent of youth identify as LGBTQ. However, 20 percent of youth in juvenile justice facilities identify as LGBTQ.[10]

The report notes that the discrepancy is a result of discrimination, such as family rejection, homelessness, and unsafe schools. LGBTQ youth also face discrimination throughout the legal process. For instance, after committing nonviolent offenses such as running away or skipping school, LGBTQ youth are twice as likely as non-LGBTQ youth to be put in jail or another correctional site.

Transgender and gender-nonconforming youth who are sentenced to serve time in a facility face an additional challenge. Their gender identity is not usually taken into consideration. Rather, the juvenile justice system places them in facilities based on the sex indicated on their birth certificates.

THE QUEER DETAINEE EMPOWERMENT PROJECT

Once they are released from immigration detention facilities, LGBTQ people have few places to turn to for resources such as housing, education, legal assistance, and emotional support. In New York City, the Queer Detainee Empowerment Project (QDEP) aids people who have left these facilities. QDEP also advocates for various causes, such as ending solitary confinement, increasing access for asylum seekers, and reforming the bail bond process for LGBTQ people.

Furthermore, workers are more likely to separate these youths from the general population and into segregated areas or solitary confinement. This separation can be harmful. Research shows that isolating young people increases their likelihood of suicide.

As awareness of the needs of the LGBTQ community, including those of LGBTQ youth, continues to grow, some states have made efforts to improve their juvenile justice systems. In Massachusetts, for example, every employee of its juvenile justice department participates in training for working with LGBTQ youth. In New York City, trans inmates can choose which gender to be housed with. California's Santa Clara County has also changed its juvenile justice system, focusing on policy, training, and involving families. These policies can help improve acceptance

ALYSSA RODRIGUEZ FIGHTS BACK

Alyssa Rodriguez spent time in New York's juvenile justice system, including a male facility. Rodriguez is transgender. The state placed her based on her sex assigned at birth. In addition, the state would not let Rodriguez take her prescription hormone medication, and workers punished Rodriguez for expressing her gender identity. She suffered physically and emotionally. In 2006, Rodriguez sued the New York Office of Children and Family Services. She won. As a result, the state has specified two of its juvenile facilities as being for LGBTQ youth. The people who work at them have received training to help them help youth who have suffered trauma.

and mental health and lower the rates of homelessness and incarceration for LGBTQ youth. According to Carmelyn Malalis, the chair and commissioner of the New York City Commission on Human Rights, "Respecting someone's gender identity or gender expression is key in making sure that everyone . . . is living with dignity and respect. The fact that somebody's incarcerated or not doesn't really change that."[11]

DISCUSSION STARTERS

- Why might LGBTQ youth who are incarcerated have a difficult time advocating for their rights?

- What are some ways that your race, gender, and sexuality intersect?

8

LOOKING
AHEAD

The social landscape continues to change, and so does the legal landscape. As the United States is increasingly confronted by demands for equality for LGBTQ people, individuals and lawmakers alike must face the reality that not every person fits—or should fit—what has long been considered "normal."

ANTI-LGBTQ EDUCATION LAWS

Several issues exist that affect LGBTQ people generally and LGBTQ youth specifically. One is censorship in school. As of March 2019, seven states had laws limiting LGBTQ topics in school. Sometimes referred to as "Don't Say Gay" or "No Promo Homo" laws, the various pieces of legislation define what teachers can discuss with students regarding LGBTQ topics. For instance, Alabama, Louisiana, Oklahoma, Mississippi, South Carolina, and Texas have laws regarding health class. Most of them make talking about LGBTQ sexual health illegal.

Oklahoma's law mandates that HIV/AIDS education state that "engaging in homosexual activity" is "primarily responsible for contact with the AIDS virus."[1] This is false information. While some people in the LGBTQ community are more likely to contract HIV than people not in the LGBTQ community due to other risk factors, a person's sexual orientation or gender identity is not responsible if they contract the virus.

Some states are changing policies about LGBTQ education in school. In March 2017, after a lawsuit against the state by three students and the organization Equality Utah, Utah overturned its anti-LGBTQ education law. One issue with the previous law was that it prohibited supporting LGBTQ issues. In one instance, students bullied a seven-year-old

MOVING IN THE OPPOSITE DIRECTION

Acceptance for LGBTQ Americans has risen for several years. However, in 2017, research found that for the first time since 2014, acceptance declined. The study, conducted by GLAAD and the Harris Poll, found that 79 percent of Americans believed LGBTQ people deserved equal rights. That stayed the same from the previous year. However, more people reported that they would feel uncomfortable if they had LGBTQ neighbors or saw a same-sex couple holding hands. John Gerzema, the CEO of the Harris Poll, stated that some people are taking the current political climate as justification to express their discomfort with LGBTQ people. Survey respondents gave the "PC response" that they supported equal rights but also said they would be uncomfortable with LGBTQ family members. According to Gerzema, "When it comes to walking the walk of LGBTQ acceptance, it seems like Americans are pulling back."[2]

Some schools regulate students' gender expressions in their dress code policies. For example, the policy may state that students assigned male at birth may not wear makeup.

boy because he sometimes wore clothes traditionally intended for girls. The anti-LGBTQ education law prohibited teachers and staff from saying it was acceptable for boys to wear girls' clothing. The law did not create a safe environment for LGBTQ students. Now, said Clifford Rosky of Equality Utah, "Every student in Utah public schools is entitled to an education free from all manner of bullying or discrimination."[3]

GENDER IDENTITY BILLS

Gender identity and bathroom use has been a hot issue for some people in the United States. In 2016, several states considered banning transgender people from using the bathroom that conforms with their identity.

TRANSGENDER MILITARY SERVICE MEMBERS

For many people, joining the armed forces is a part of growing up. But in 2017, President Trump issued a memo banning trans people from serving in the military. This ban stopped trans recruits from enlisting.

However, not every branch decided to uphold the ban. California's National Guard decided to go against the ban in 2019. One leader in the National Guard, Major General Matthew Beevers, said, "As long as you fight, we don't care what gender you identify as." He went on to assure transgender service members who underwent gender confirmation surgery that "nobody's going to kick [them] out."[5]

The topic caused a heated debate in South Carolina in particular. While politicians such as Lee Bright, a senator in South Carolina, pushed for a "bathroom bill," others challenged the idea. In Tennessee, leaders from companies such as Dow Chemical, T-Mobile, and Williams-Sonoma signed a letter asking legislators not to create a "bathroom bill." And in Louisiana, the governor officially banned discrimination against LGBTQ people in state government.

In March 2016, North Carolina became the first state to pass a "bathroom bill." It is the only state to have done so. North Carolina governor Roy Cooper spoke with CNN in March 2017 about the law, describing it as "a dark cloud hanging over our great state. It has stained our reputation. It has discriminated against our people and it has caused great economic harm in many of our communities."[4] Because of its "bathroom bill,"

North Carolina lost out on a variety of business opportunities, including concerts and conventions. On March 30, 2017, North Carolina repealed its "bathroom bill." However, the new law prevented both state and local governments from regulating bathroom access. This meant that local governments still could not pass legislation regarding bathrooms. LGBTQ supporters saw the new law as still anti-LGBTQ and not actually a repeal.

Other states have taken steps to fight discrimination. As of June 2018, 18 states and Washington, DC, had passed laws against transgender discrimination in bathrooms, as well as in employment and housing. In addition, more than 200 cities had passed similar rules.

TITLE IX

LGBTQ students could be affected another way, through Title IX. Title IX is a civil rights law. It prohibits discrimination based on sex by schools that receive money from the federal government.

The federal government has made the bathroom issue less clear. In 2016, the federal government told US public schools to let students use the bathroom that corresponds with their gender identity. However, in 2017, under a new administration led by Donald Trump, the government abolished that guideline. Instead, it would be up to the states and to school districts to determine bathroom policies. In addition, the US Department of Education would no longer investigate complaints by transgender students about not being able to use the bathroom that fits their gender.

Secretary of Education Betsy DeVos pushed for the government's change on transgender bathroom usage. After ending the bathroom protection for transgender students, DeVos expressed support for LGBTQ students: "All schools must ensure that all students, including LGBT students, are able to learn and thrive in a safe environment."[6]

Even with this statement, LGBTQ advocates are concerned about the message the Trump administration is sending. Schools that do not already have policies in place may think they should ban transgender students from the bathrooms and locker rooms that correspond with their identities.

EJ JOHNSON

EJ Johnson was outed by the tabloid *TMZ* in 2013. Johnson is comfortable with his gay identity. However, he was uncomfortable with all the questions and assumptions that came with being outed. Johnson was a reality TV star on *Rich Kids of Beverly Hills*. Even though Johnson identifies as a cis gay man, he embraces a gender-neutral presentation. He likes wearing makeup and jewelry—things that are typically seen as feminine. At a 2017 Beautycon panel, Johnson said, "That's just the way we're moving in the world, where everyone's just going to be one big gray area."[7]

Youth are the future of the LGBTQ community.

TEACHERS IN NIXA PUSH FOR CHANGE

When Michael Sadowski spoke with NPR about *Safe Is Not Enough: Better Schools for LGBTQ Students*, he shared stories from his book about what he calls "turning adversity into activism." One story was about teachers in Nixa, Missouri, who were trying to create a more LGBTQ-inclusive curriculum. Teachers wanted students to read the book *My Two Moms*. Written by Zach Wahls, it tells his story of growing up with two mothers, a same-sex couple.

The teachers were met with anti-LGBTQ reactions from several students and by people in the community. The teachers also did not have much support from the school administration. The teachers' request was denied. When that happened, the teachers arranged for Wahls to visit Nixa and take part in a community discussion. Approximately 300 people attended. The teachers also took students to the state capitol to meet with leaders who have spoken negatively about GSAs and to push for antibullying legislation. For Sadowski, this work is invaluable. He said, "Kids should never have to deal with negative messages about who they are from their parents or their peers or their religious or political leaders. But the teachers at Nixa are showing their students that if this happens, there are ways to respond that can lead to real change."[9]

FINDING HOPE

The HRC began its 2018 report by stating that though tremendous strides have been made in equality and inclusion in the previous decade, there is still room for improvement for "LGBTQ-identified youth in terms of acceptance and support from their families, their mental health and safety in schools." Additionally, the HRC noted that "for LGBTQ youth of color these challenges are compounded by racism and race-related stressors."[8]

These words could leave someone feeling discouraged, even hopeless. But hope exists in chosen families and beyond. Changes continue to take place, such as increasing numbers of LGBTQ characters in the media and LGBTQ content and communities online. According to the HRC, "Across the country, LGBTQ youth are taking a stand and advocating for inclusivity and equality in their homes, schools and communities."[10]

Progress happens and will keep happening because of the determination and dedication of LGBTQ youth, various organizations, supportive families and friends, and government institutions. Every voice matters and can make a positive difference. Growing up LGBTQ is not always easy, but it can get better.

DISCUSSION STARTERS

- Should bathrooms in school be separated into boys' and girls' bathrooms? Why or why not?

- Why do you think acceptance for LGBTQ students is moving forward in some respects but not in others?

- What are some ways that you can get involved with politics in your community? How might you advocate for the rights of LGBTQ youth?

ESSENTIAL FACTS

SIGNIFICANT EVENTS

- In 2017, the Human Rights Campaign (HRC) conducted a survey of lesbian, gay, bisexual, transgender, and queer (LGBTQ) youth. Respondents reported how they felt about safety in school, parental support, and other factors. These responses helped shape the HRC's future policies regarding LGBTQ youth.

- Beginning with the Trump administration in 2017, the US Department of Education refused to hear Title IX complaints from trans students seeking to use bathrooms that correspond with their gender identities.

KEY PLAYERS

- The Gay, Lesbian, and Straight Education Network (GLSEN) advocates for LGBTQ youth in schools and elsewhere. It provides resources to youth such as information on starting gay-straight alliances (GSAs) and tips for discussing sexuality and gender identity with teachers and peers.

- Sage Lovell was elected to the homecoming court in her Georgia high school. She became the first trans person elected to homecoming court in Georgia history.

- Byshop Elliott filed a lawsuit against McKinley High School in 2017 because students could not purchase tickets for their same-sex prom dates. After the lawsuit, the school allowed same-sex couples to attend school dances, including prom.

IMPACT ON SOCIETY

How people grow up determines their successes later in life. People in the LGBTQ community have different experiences than non-LGBTQ people. Some gay and lesbian students fight to bring their same-sex dates to school dances, while some trans students fight to use the restrooms and locker rooms that align with their gender identities. However, LGBTQ youth succeed when they create their own support systems, such as GSAs at school and communities of other LGBTQ people known as "found families." Through education, awareness, and support, people who are growing up LGBTQ can have positive experiences that shape their adulthood.

QUOTE

"I think being open with myself has made me prouder of my identity as a queer person. I know that. Regardless of what others think of my sexual orientation, I am able to love who I love and not be ashamed of it."

—Anonymous survey respondent, 2017 HRC youth survey

GLOSSARY

ADVERSE
Unfavorable or hostile.

CISGENDER (CIS)
Having a gender identity that matches the sex they were assigned at birth.

DRAG
An art and performance style that involves a performer dressing and acting as a gender that is not their own.

DRAG KING
A performer, usually a cisgender woman, who dresses as a man for the purpose of entertaining others at bars, clubs, or other events.

DRAG QUEEN
A performer, usually a cisgender man, who dresses as a woman for the purpose of entertaining others at bars, clubs, or other events.

GENDER DYSPHORIA
The distress caused by having a gender identity that does not match the sex assigned at birth.

GENDER EXPRESSION
The outward appearance of someone's gender identity.

GENDER IDENTITY

A person's perception of their gender, which may or may not correspond with the sex they were assigned at birth.

HORMONE REPLACEMENT THERAPY

A drug regimen for some trans people that introduces estrogen or testosterone into the body to change its appearance.

INCARCERATION

The state of being in prison.

NONBINARY

Having a gender identity that is neither male nor female, or sometimes both male and female.

SEXUAL ORIENTATION

A person's identity in relation to the gender(s) they find sexually attractive.

TRANSGENDER (TRANS)

Having a gender identity that does not match the sex they were assigned at birth.

ADDITIONAL RESOURCES

SELECTED BIBLIOGRAPHY

Balingit, Moriah. "Education Department No Longer Investigating Transgender Bathroom Complaints." *Washington Post*, 12 Feb. 2018, washingtonpost.com. Accessed 25 Feb. 2019.

"The History of Coming Out." *Human Rights Campaign*, n.d., hrc.org. Accessed 25 Feb. 2019.

"2017 National School Climate Survey." *GLSEN*, 2018, glsen.org. Accessed 25 Feb. 2019.

FURTHER READINGS

Bronski, Michael L. *A Queer History of the United States for Young People*. Beacon, 2019.

Cook, Maria. *Gender Identity: Beyond Pronouns and Bathrooms*. Nomad, 2019.

Harris, Duchess, and Kristin Marciniak. *Being Transgender in America*. Abdo, 2020.

ONLINE RESOURCES

To learn more about growing up LGBTQ, please visit **abdobooklinks.com** or scan this QR code. These links are routinely monitored and updated to provide the most current information available.

MORE INFORMATION

For more information on this subject, contact or visit the following organizations:

CENTER FOR AMERICAN PROGRESS
1333 H St. NW, Tenth Floor
Washington, DC 20005
americanprogress.org

The Center for American Progress is an independent, nonpartisan policy institute with progressive ideals. It aims to shape policies regarding education, LGBTQ issues, immigration, and poverty through public action and media coverage.

HUMAN RIGHTS CAMPAIGN
1640 Rhode Island Ave. NW
Washington, DC 20036-3278
hrc.org

The Human Rights Campaign (HRC) is the largest LGBTQ civil rights organization in the United States. Its mission is to inspire and engage individuals and communities to end LGBTQ discrimination.

MOVEMENT ADVANCEMENT PROJECT
3020 Carbon Pl., Suite 202
Boulder, CO 80301
lgbtmap.org

The Movement Advancement Project (MAP) is an independent organization focused on achieving equal rights for the LGBTQ population. Its website offers research and insight about many issues facing the LGBTQ community.

SOURCE NOTES

CHAPTER 1. HOMECOMING FOR SAGE LOVELL

1. Charlene Adams. "Transgender Teen First in the State of Georgia to Be Elected to High School's Homecoming Court." *Daily Mail*, 18 Oct. 2014, dailymail.co.uk. Accessed 25 Mar. 2019.

2. Sarah Kate Ellis. "Southern Stories." *GLAAD*, n.d., glaad.org. Accessed 25 Mar. 2019.

3. Claire Pires. "All Access: First Trans Teen on Homecoming Court in Georgia." *GLAAD*, 6 Nov. 2014, glaad.org. Accessed 25 Mar. 2019.

4. Ross Murray. "#SouthernStories for #GivingTuesday: Sage Lovell." *GLAAD*, 2 Dec. 2014, glaad.org. Accessed 25 Mar. 2019.

5. Murray, "#SouthernStories for #GivingTuesday."

6. Patrick Saunders. "Transgender East Cobb Teen Re-elected to Homecoming Court." *Georgia Voice*, 20 Oct. 2015, thegavoice.com. Accessed 25 Mar. 2019.

7. Murray, "#SouthernStories for #GivingTuesday."

CHAPTER 2. WHAT IT MEANS TO BE LGBTQ

1. "The Term Same Gender Loving." *Urban Socialites*, 4 Dec. 2012, urbansocialities.com. Accessed 25 Mar. 2019.

2. Riese Bernard. "Hayley Kiyoko: American Teen Lesbian Heartthrob." *Nylon*, 1 June 2018, nylon.com. Accessed 5 Apr. 2019.

3. @MerriamWebster. "People keep 1) saying they don't know what 'genderqueer' means . . ." *Twitter*, 25 Apr. 2016, 10:05 a.m., twitter.com. Accessed 25 Mar. 2019.

4. Avianne Tan. "Merriam-Webster Adds 'Genderqueer,' 'Genderfluid' and Gender Neutral Title 'Mx' to Dictionary." *ABC News*, 26 Apr. 2016, abcnews.go.com. Accessed 25 Mar. 2019.

5. Emma Sarran Webster. "Brandon Studler Discusses Life as the Only Openly Transgender Person Working on Capitol Hill." *Teen Vogue*, 29 June 2018, teenvogue.com. Accessed 25 Mar. 2019.

6. @elierlick. "Are we still doing the 2012 vs 2017 thing? . . ." *Instagram*, 24 Oct. 2017, instagram.com. Accessed 25 Mar. 2019.

7. Katie Van Syckle. "As Far as Fashion Went, I Always Wanted to Be in a Suit and a Tie." *The Cut*, 26 Feb. 2016, thecut.com. Accessed 25 Mar. 2019.

8. Cassie Donish. "Five Queer People on What 'Femme' Means to Them." *Vice*, 4 Dec. 2017, vice.com. Accessed 25 Mar. 2019.

9. Lauren Booker. "What It Means to Be Gender-Fluid." *CNN*, 13 Apr. 2016, cnn.com. Accessed 25 Mar. 2019.

10. Sassafras Lowrey. "A Guide to Non-Binary Pronouns and Why They Matter." *Huffpost*, 8 Nov. 2017, huffingtonpost.com. Accessed 25 Mar. 2019.

CHAPTER 3. FIGHTING SOCIETAL NORMS

1. Lauren Booker. "What It Means to Be Gender-Fluid." *CNN*, 13 Apr. 2016, cnn.com. Accessed 25 Mar. 2019.

2. Booker, "What It Means to Be Gender-Fluid."

3. Olivia Rudgard. "Only Two Thirds of Generation Z Identify as 'Exclusively Heterosexual.'" *Telegraph*, 5 July 2018, telegraph.co.uk. Accessed 25 Mar. 2019.

4. Gary J. Gates. "How Many People Are Lesbian, Gay, Bisexual, and Transgender." *Williams Institute*, Apr. 2011, williamsinstitute.law.ucla.edu. Accessed 25 Mar. 2019.

5. Heather Leah. "'A' Is for Asexual: Erasing the Asexual Orientation." *HuffPost*, 17 June 2017, huffingtonpost.com. Accessed 25 Mar. 2019.

6. "Glossary of Terms - Lesbian/Gay/Bisexual/Queer." *GLAAD*, n.d., glaad.org. Accessed 25 Mar. 2019.

7. Charlotte Dingle. "13 Things You Should Know before Dating a Bi Girl." *Cosmopolitan*, 11 Dec. 2015, cosmopolitan.com. Accessed 25 Mar. 2019.

8. Lisa Wade. "Five Reasons Why Gendered Products Are a Problem." *Society Pages*, 31 Dec. 2015, thesocietypages.org. Accessed 25 Mar. 2019.

9. Booker, "What It Means to Be Gender-Fluid."

10. Bill de Blasio and Julie Menin. "From Cradle to Cane: The Cost of Being a Female Consumer." *NYC Consumer Affairs*, Dec. 2015, nyc.gov. Accessed 25 Mar. 2019.

11. de Blasio and Menin, "From Cradle to Cane."

CHAPTER 4. COMING OUT

1. Kassandra Brabaw. "What We Mean When We Talk about Coming Out (of the Closet)." *Refinery29*, 11 Oct. 2018, refinery29.com. Accessed 25 Mar. 2019.

2. Evan Urquhart. "'Most of the Time People Don't Recognize Me at All.'" *Slate*, 29 June 2018, slate.com. Accessed 25 Mar. 2019.

3. Dawn Ennis. "10 Words Transgender People Want You to Know (But Not Say)." *Advocate*, 4 Feb. 2016, advocate.com. Accessed 25 Mar. 2019.

4. Laila Ibrahim. "Coming Out Again . . . and Again . . . and Again." *HuffPost*, 10 June 2017, huffingtonpost.com. Accessed 25 Mar. 2019.

5. University of Washington Counseling Center. "Thinking of Coming Out?" *University of Washington*, n.d., washington.edu. Accessed 25 Mar. 2019.

6. Cameron Wallace. "Social Media Is Critical to LGBTQ Youth—But Not for the Reasons You Might Think." *OutSmart Magazine*, 28 June 2017, outsmartmagazine.com. Accessed 25 Mar. 2019.

7. Carol Kuruvilla. "Chilling Study Sums Up Link between Religion and Suicide for Queer Youth." *HuffPost*, 18 Apr. 2018, huffingtonpost.com. Accessed 25 Mar. 2019.

8. Alexis Blue. "LGBT Teens Who Come Out at School Are Happier." *Futurity*, 11 Oct. 2017, futurity.org. Accessed 25 Mar. 2019.

9. "2018 LGBTQ Youth Report." *Human Rights Campaign*, 2018, hrc.org. Accessed 25 Mar. 2019.

10. "Tips for Parents of LGBTQ Youth." *Johns Hopkins Medicine*, n.d., hopkinsmedicine.org. Accessed 25 Mar. 2019.

11. "2018 LGBTQ Youth Report."

12. "Overcoming Low Self-Esteem and Inner Homophobia." *Gay Therapy Center*, n.d., thegaytherapycenter.com. Accessed 25 Mar. 2019.

13. Lindsey Jacobson. "What Is National Coming Out Day?" *ABC News*, 11 Oct. 2018, abcnews.go.com. Accessed 25 Mar. 2019.

14. Ric Chollar. "10 Physical and Emotional Health Concerns of LGBTQ Students." *Campus Pride*, 17 June 2013, campuspride.org. Accessed 25 Mar. 2019.

15. Michael Blackmon. "Samira Wiley Said She 'Cried a Lot' . . ." *BuzzFeed News*, 9 Oct. 2018, buzzfeednews.com. Accessed 5 Apr. 2019.

16. Jeff Ingold. "Why It's Never Okay to Out Someone." *Stonewall*, 27 Mar. 2018, stonewall.org.uk. Accessed 1 Apr. 2019.

17. JM Wilkerson, et al. "Social Support, Depression, Self-Esteem, and Coping among LGBTQ Adolescents Participating in Hatch Youth." *Health Promotion Practice*, May 2017, issue 18, vol. 3. 358–365. Accessed 25 Mar. 2019.

18. "Tips for Parents of LGBTQ Youth."

19. "Tips for Parents of LGBTQ Youth."

SOURCE NOTES
CONTINUED

CHAPTER 5. THE SCHOOL EXPERIENCE

1. "2018 LGBTQ Youth Report." *Human Rights Campaign*, 2018, hrc.org. Accessed 25 Mar. 2019.

2. "2018 LGBTQ Youth Report."

3. Marissa Higgins. "LGBT Students Are Not Safe at School." *Atlantic*, 18 Oct. 2016, theatlantic.com. Accessed 25 Mar. 2019.

4. Minyvonne Burke. "Girl Who Asked Her Girlfriend to Prom . . ." *Daily Mail*, 2 Feb. 2018, dailymail.co.uk. Accessed 25 Mar. 2019.

5. Ben Kesslen. "Two Percent of High School Students Identify as Transgender, CDC Report Finds." *NBC News*, 24 Jan. 2019, nbcnews.com. Accessed 25 Mar. 2019.

6. Brenda Álvarez. "'I'm a Normal Kid': Transgender Students Thrive in Supportive Schools." *NEAToday*, 15 Nov. 2016, neatoday.org. Accessed 25 Mar. 2019.

7. Associated Press. "LGBTQ Teens in West Virginia Create State's First 'Rainbow' Prom." *NBC News*, 23 Apr. 2018, nbcnews.com. Accessed 25 Mar. 2019.

8. Associated Press, "LGBTQ Teens in West Virginia Create State's First 'Rainbow' Prom."

9. Higgins, "LGBT Students Are Not Safe at School."

10. Higgins, "LGBT Students Are Not Safe at School."

11. "2018 LGBTQ Youth Report."

12. Kendra Yoshinaga. "For LGBTQ Students, Author Says, Safety Is 'Not Enough.'" *NPR*, 14 July 2016, npr.org. Accessed 25 Mar. 2019.

CHAPTER 6. FINDING FAMILY AND ROLE MODELS

1. Kyle Casey Chu. "Why Queer People Need Chosen Families." *Vice*, 13 Nov. 2017, vice.com. Accessed 25 Mar. 2019.

2. Jacob Tobia. "Queer 2.0: The Importance of 'Chosen Family.'" *NBC News*, 17 Nov. 2016, nbcnews.com. Accessed 25 Mar. 2019.

3. Tobia, "Queer 2.0."

4. Chu, "Why Queer People Need Chosen Families."

5. John Paul Brammer. "LGBTQ and Out on Social Media—But Nowhere Else." *NBC News*, 11 Oct. 2017, nbcnews.com. Accessed 25 Mar. 2019.

6. "Chosen Family 2018 Year in Review." *A Better Balance*, 19 Dec. 2018, abetterbalance.org. Accessed 25 Mar. 2019.

7. "Our Work." *GLAAD*, n.d., glaad.org. Accessed 25 Mar. 2019.

8. "LGBT Representations on Television Lacking Diversity . . ." *GLAAD*, n.d., glaad.org. Accessed 25 Mar. 2019.

9. "Where We Are on TV Report - 2017." *GLAAD*, 2018, glaad.org. Accessed 25 Mar. 2019.

10. Joe Otterson. "'Pose' Renewed for Season 2 at FX." *Variety*, 12 July 2018, variety.com. Accessed 25 Mar. 2019.

11. Eva Reign. "Queer Eye's Fab Five Reminds Me of Chosen Family." *Them*, 16 June 2018, them.us. Accessed 25 Mar. 2019.

12. Reign, "Queer Eye's Fab Five Reminds Me of Chosen Family."

13. "Tyler Oakley." *Out*, n.d., out.com. Accessed 25 Mar. 2019.

CHAPTER 7. THE CHALLENGES OF DISCRIMINATION

1. Shabab Ahmed Mirza and Caitlin Rooney. "Discrimination Prevents LGBTQ People from Accessing Health Care." *Center for American Progress*, 18 Jan. 2018, americanprogress.org. Accessed 25 Mar. 2019.

2. Ryan Thoreson. "'You Don't Want Second Best': Anti-LGBT Discrimination in US Health Care." *Human Rights Watch*, n.d., hrw.org. Accessed 19 Mar. 2019.

3. Natalia Deeb-Sossa et al. "Building Partnerships" *UC Davis Center for Reducing Health Disparities*, June 2009, health.ucdavis.edu. Accessed 25 Mar. 2019.

4. "Unjust." *Center for American Progress and Movement Advancement Project*, Aug. 2016, lgbtmap.org. Accessed 25 Mar. 2019.

5. Chapin Hall. "Missed Opportunities: Youth Homelessness in America." *Voices of Youth Count*, 2017, voicesofyouthcount.org. Accessed 25 Mar. 2019.

6. "LGBTQ Youth in the Foster Care System." *Human Rights Campaign*, n.d., hrc.org. Accessed 25 Mar. 2019.

7. "LGBT Homelessness." *National Coalition for the Homeless*, n.d., nationalhomeless.org. Accessed 25 Mar. 2019.

8. Christianna Silva. "LGBT Youth Are 120% More Likely to Be Homeless Than Straight People, Study Shows." *Newsweek*, 30 Nov. 2017, newsweek.com. Accessed 25 Mar. 2019.

9. Michael Lyle. "Transgender Homeless Struggle to Find Shelter, Resources." *Nevada Current*, 20 July 2018, nevadacurrent.com. Accessed 25 Mar. 2019.

10. "Unjust."

11. Rich Calder. "Transgender Inmates Can Now Choose Where They're Housed in NYC." *New York Post*, 16 Apr. 2018, nypost.com. Accessed 25 Mar. 2019.

CHAPTER 8. LOOKING AHEAD

1. Corinne Segal. "Eight States Censor LGBTQ Topics in School. Now, a Lawsuit Is Challenging That." *PBS*, 29 Jan. 2017, pbs.org. Accessed 25 Mar. 2019.

2. Alyssa Rosenberg. "In Three Years, LGBT Americans Have Gone from Triumph to Backlash."

3. Lindsay Whitehurst. "Case over LGBT Talk in Schools Settled after Utah Law Change." *Deseret News Utah*, 6 Oct. 2017, deseretnews.com

4. Yezmin Villarreal. "Here's All the Business N.C. Has Lost because of Anti-LGBT Bill." *Advocate*, 13 Apr. 2016, advocate.com. Accessed 25 Mar. 2019.

5. Adam Ashton. "California National Guard to Transgender Troops: 'Nobody's Going to Kick You Out.'" *Fresno Bee*, 6 Feb. 2019, fresnobee.com. Accessed 25 Mar. 2019.

6. Moriah Balingit. "Education Department No Longer Investigating Transgender Bathroom Complaints." *Washington Post*, 12 Feb. 2018, washingtonpost.com. Accessed 25 Mar. 2019.

7. Michael Schulman. "EJ Johnson Is 'Not Just Some Other Rich Girl.'" *New York Times*, 2 Sept. 2017, nytimes.com. Accessed 25 Mar. 2019.

8. Human Rights Campaign. "Growing Up LGBT in America." *Human Rights Campaign*, 2012, hrc.org. Accessed 19 Mar. 2019.

9. Kendra Yoshinaga. "For LGBTQ Students, Author Says, Safety Is 'Not Enough.'" *NPR*, 14 July 2016, npr.org. Accessed 25 Mar. 2019.

10. "2018 LGBTQ Youth Report." *Human Rights Campaign*, 2018, hrc.org. Accessed 25 Mar. 2019.

INDEX

ABOUT THE AUTHORS

DUCHESS HARRIS, JD, PHD

Dr. Harris is a professor of American Studies at Macalester College and curator of the Duchess Harris Collection of ABDO books. She is also the coauthor of the titles in the collection, which features popular selections such as *Hidden Human Computers: The Black Women of NASA* and series including News Literacy and Being Female in America.

Before working with ABDO, Dr. Harris authored several other books on the topics of race, culture, and American history. She served as an associate editor for *Litigation News*, the American Bar Association Section of Litigation's quarterly flagship publication, and was the first editor in chief of *Law Raza*, an interactive online journal covering race and the law, published at William Mitchell College of Law. She has earned a PhD in American Studies from the University of Minnesota and a JD from William Mitchell College of Law.

REBECCA ROWELL

As an editor and as an author working on dozens of books, Rebecca Rowell has put her degree in publishing and writing to work. Recent topics as an author include the American middle class and the Paris climate agreement. She lives in Minneapolis, Minnesota.